NICE

The ANTI ANXIETY WORKBOOK

Love

GOOD DAY!

Welcome. . .

And congratulations!

Because if you have this book in your hands, it means that you have decided to change, to move forward and to stop suffering from anxiety. And if someone gave you this book, it means you have good friends!

This book is a toolbox.

You will find :

- Exercises to understand the mechanisms of anxiety and its impact on your body and mind.

- Exercises to understand your own functioning and to free yourself from worries.

- Simple tips and fun exercises for light stress management on a daily basis

- Practices for long-term stress management.

- Exercises to develop your self-confidence.

- Coloring pages to help you relax.

About the author

Who am I? Is it that important? Maybe I am you?

First of all, you should know that I am not a psychologist, I am not a doctor, I am not a guru.

I am a man, born in the 80s. I have done many things in my life. I've had different jobs, in very different fields. I have played several sports, and I have been interested in many passions. I have met many different people.

What you need to know about me is that I am a very anxious person. I have lived with this since my childhood. I have suffered from the torments of anxiety for years.

I've always tried to improve myself, both in my professional and personal life. And anxiety was a formidable enemy that kept me from moving forward.

So I said STOP.

For years, I observed my behaviors and those of others. I studied, I tested practices, I studied again. I understood and learned many things. As I had trained a lot, and even obtained some nice diplomas, I became a business coach for a while.

And if there was only one thing to remember, it's that we are responsible for our anxiety. A second thing to remember? Anxiety never goes away. Don't expect a miracle or divine intervention, and don't rely on medication. But the good news is that you can control your anxiety. And it's not that complicated. In fact, it's like learning to play the guitar (or piano, for that matter). You can't just pick up a guitar for the first time and play a complicated melody. You'll have to practice, over and over again. Controlling your anxiety, your stress, is the same thing.

That's what I propose in this book: lots of little exercises to understand and control your anxiety. You will find that some of them correspond to you, others not. This is normal, each person is different. What I ask is that you try each exercise, several times if possible. Again, there is no miracle. Give yourself time. Consider this book as a beginning, as the first (often the most difficult) step. And above all, keep in mind this quote: The best way to fail? Stop before you succeed.

To contact the author : thekarmafive@gmail.com

Anxiety, that strange thing.

We all feel anxiety at one time or another. Some of us get rid of it very quickly, some of us only experience it on rare occasions. And then there are those who live with it daily, those for whom anxiety is poison. Maybe you are one of them?

But what is anxiety? There are many definitions. Some will say "it is fear". And I would say "yes and no". Anxiety is not really Fear, it's its evil twin.

Fear is a natural thing. It's the direct response to danger or threat. Fear prepares us to escape, to take a defensive posture, or even to fight.

Anxiety is an emotion directed towards the future (near or far), in which we are not ready to face negative events, most often hypothetical.

Fear lives in the present, Anxiety lives in the future.
Fear is linked to a real situation, Anxiety is not.

Imagine...

You are watching television quietly. Suddenly a spider appears right there, next to you. You jump, you run away, you scream. This is Fear.

But imagine this...

You are watching television quietly. Quietly? Really? No, because you're always looking around you. The walls, the ceiling, under the sofa. Why? In case a spider appears. And you do that every day.

There is no spider. But you're afraid of it... And you are focused on that fear.

This is Anxiety.

By the way, how many times have you been anxious about something that in the end never happened?

How many times have you imagined the worst, when it never happened?

Meditate on it.

War. . .

""If you know the enemy and know yourself, you need not fear the result of a hundred battles. If you know yourself but not the enemy, for every victory gained you will also suffer a defeat. If you know neither the enemy nor yourself, you will succumb in every battle."

Sun Tzu, The Art of War

Yes, we are going to go to war.

But it's a peaceful war.

There will be no brutality or violence.

On the contrary, we will go to war smiling, with love!

In reality, this war, this fight, is against ourselves. Anxiety is an enemy that we have created ourselves. It's inside us. We are certainly not going to start a murderous war and try to kill anxiety. After all, it's a part of us.

In fact, we are going to tame it, and learn to live with it, in serenity.

But even if this fight is peaceful, it's still a fight! And a fight requires concentration, training, sometimes a little suffering, to live better, to live free.

And Peace!

As Sun Tzu says so well, we must know our enemy as well as we know ourselves.

Understand that you must therefore know who you are, deep down inside.

Understand also that you must know your enemy, and understand his strategy.

Are you ready for this war?

Yes ?

Then let's go.

Take your weapons: Your smile, your good mood, and above all your love.

Declaration of War

The first step is to declare war on anxiety. Remember, a peaceful war.

So in this first exercise we are going to write to our anxiety.

Explain that it has become too invasive and that you cannot live with it in peace.

Explain what it does to you and how it affects you in your life.

Explain that you want your freedom back and what you will get out of it.

Explain that you regret having been in this situation for so long. Forgive your ennemy, and forgive yourself, because YOU have created this little monster, this dictator of your emotions.

Explain that you will fight it, with LOVE but with STRENGTH.

Write down your declaration of WAR

Dear Anxiety

My Body

Anxiety acts on our body, and it's important to identify its effects accurately.

For many people, stress acts differently depending on its cause.

For me, if something frightens me (a meeting, an appointment), I have nausea.
If I'm angry, then I have a stiff neck.

Identifying the effects on our body will help us to prevent stress.

Do you have muscle tension? Try yoga, Qigong.

Do you have stomach aches? Try breathing exercises.

Don't hesitate to talk to your doctor, who will be able to advise you.

Identify the areas of your body that are impacted by stress.

And have fun! If you have a headache, draw a flower on your forehead. Do you have a stomach ache? Draw a little cloud on your belly.

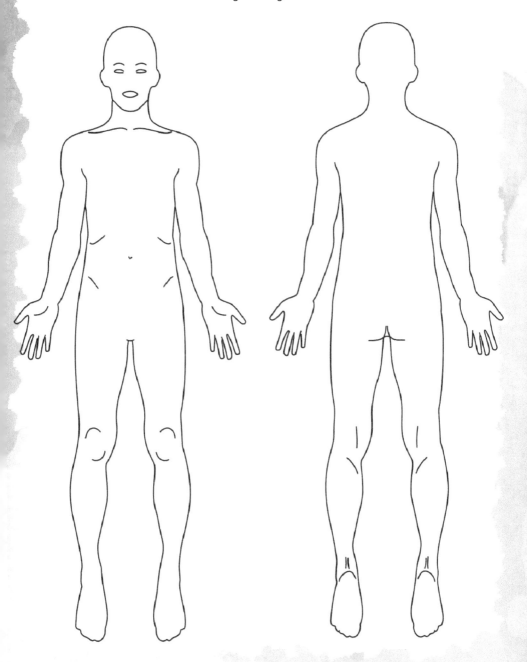

My Worries Bag

We all have worries, and we carry them every day. And often we add to them, again and again.

Our "Worries Bag" gets heavier and heavier.

It's time to open it and see what's inside. That's the first step in cleaning up.

List all the worries you have in your bag.

My Worries Bag

Anti-Worry Playlist

Music is a very interesting tool for keeping negative emotions, anxiety and gloom at bay.

Whatever your musical tastes are, whether you like rock or classical music, hip hop or pop. Just one instruction: No sad music!

Create your anti-worry playlist now.

Take your music with you wherever you can. A little moment of anxiety?

Play the music!

My anti-worry playlist

don't let the world change your smile but let your smile change the world.

My Personal Values

Our personal values are our pillars. They guide our choices and actions, and give meaning to our lives. They are a formidable weapon against stress!

Our personal values help us focus on the important things. They help us to focus on ourselves. The more you know yourself, the stronger you are.

In concrete terms, **a personal value is a moral rule**. Everyone has their own values, and everyone gives a specific meaning to those values.

Take for example the value of honesty:

Does it mean being honest with oneself or with others? Does honesty mean that we allow ourselves to say everything? Does it mean that we can't stand people who are not honest? Everyone will have their own definition of honesty, and it's for each personal value.

But why would you want to know your personal values?

Well, simply to know who you really are. Knowing your values means knowing your strengths, but also your weaknesses. If honesty is one of your values, and one of your colleagues is dishonest, that's why you can't stand him, that's why he stresses you, that's why you are maybe afraid of him.

The objective of this exercise? To develop self-confidence, self-esteem and to make clear choices that make sense.

How to clearly identify your personal values?

This requires some reflection and being honest with yourself.

There are many methods, but my favorite is also the simplest in my opinion.

Ask yourself these few questions:

What makes me really happy? What do I like to do and why?

What am I really angry about?

Which people, real or imaginary, do I admire the most and why?

Which people, real or imaginary, do I hate the most and why?

TURN TO CONTINUE

My Personal Values

You must find at least 5 personal values, and 10 maximum. And you will have to develop each value, put words behind each of them.

Here is a personal example:

The most important personal value for me is Respect. For me, respect is being aware of others. Here's a concrete example: I can't stand people who try to get ahead of others in a line. It makes me angry, really. Another example? people who let their dog poop on the sidewalk. To me, it's disrespectful to others.

Now it's your turn.

It's a really important exercise, believe me. You will understand what can make you angry, but also what it has to do with your fears and anxieties. You will understand who you are.
Take the time, do this exercise as seriously as you can.

Once you have finished, and you have found your personal values, write them down in the flag.

This is your banner!

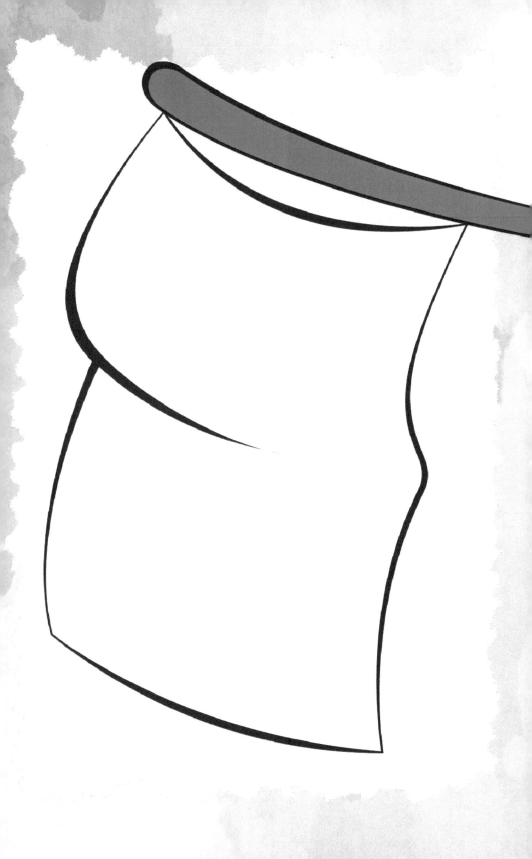

Letter to

Does a particular person make you anxious? Or does he or she make you angry?

Sometimes it's very difficult to express how we feel. So we keep our fear or anger inside, and that's very bad.

It's time to let go of it.

Write a letter to the person who is causing you the most anxiety, anger, bad feelings.

With this letter, you must explain to this person how you really feel. Be honest, be frank.

Don't just say (or write) your anger and fears. Get to the heart of your feelings. Connect them to your values.

There is no need to make him or her read it, I reassure you. Just put words to what you are feeling.

Dear . . .

A LONG TRAVEL ALWAYS BEGINS WITH THE FIRST STEP

My Fears

To be anxious is to be afraid of something. Something, but what?

This is a very interesting question.

Sometimes we are afraid of a situation, or of someone, but the real fear is elsewhere, inside us.

Are you afraid of your boss? But are you really afraid of him? Or rather, afraid of losing your job (afraid of precariousness)? Afraid of not performing (and perhaps disappointing)? Afraid of being reprimanded (and afraid of authority)? Afraid of going to talk to that beautiful boy (or girl)? Are you really afraid to talk to him/her? Or are you afraid of being rejected? Of feeling ridiculous? Are you afraid of yourself?

You see, often what we are afraid of is just a projection. Our fear is deeper inside us.

You will now have to think about everything that frightens you. Your boss? A colleague? Your mother? Dogs? Poverty? Success?

And try to find out what your real fear is.

In each cloud, write down who or what scares you. Then, in a different colour, write down your real fear.

Soap Bubbles

Here's a fun little exercise that works well for small everyday worries.

You can do it mentally, or use real soap bubbles. You know, that little toy with soap and water that bubbles when you blow on it.

Think about one of your worries. Close your eyes. Think about it really, think about it very hard. Imagine it in your mouth. Breathe in slowly.

Now open your eyes. Blow and seal the worry in a soap bubble.

Say goodbye to it and watch it fly away, far, far away.

Colour in this drawing, just for fun.

The Monster

Anxiety is like a little monster.

Give it a name! Mine is called Jack.

Jack is there, hidden inside me (or you).

Jack is not really bad. But he likes to torment me.

Jack exists because of me, because of you, at least in part.

It's time to get to know him!

Draw your little monster, give him a name.

Jack, my monster, has big scary eyes but he can't see very well. He is blue (I don't like blue) and has little claws to hold on to me. Sometimes he whispers scary things to me.

Mistakes are proof that you are trying

CATCH YOUR DREAMS

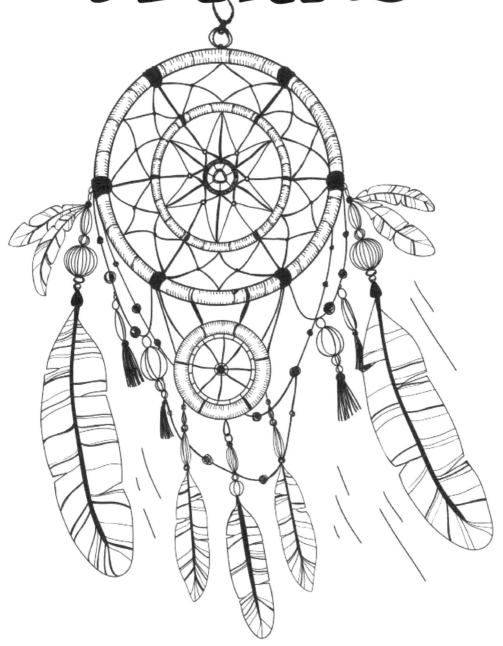

Don't feed the Monster

Often, during the day, we feed our anxiety, our stress, with a lot of little unimportant things.

Unimportant? really?

Then why do we keep them with us? Why do you still think about that guy who pissed you off on the road? Why don't you forget that unpleasant discussion with your boss? Why are you still angry about your computer problem this morning?

All these little things are really unimportant, but they are poisoning your life.

Why?

Because you think about it over and over again. Because **you feed the monster.**

Well, it's time for the monster to go on a little diet. We are going to throw away all those little unimportant things he shouldn't eat.

We need a bin.

Find a small box, or a pencil jar, or make a small cardboard bin (look on the internet, there are lots of tutorials). It should be pretty, not too big.

If possible, put it at the entrance of your house or on your desk.

Prepare small pieces of paper and a pencil.

When a small unimportant thing causes you stress or anxiety, write it down on a piece of paper. Look at it.

Are you really going to feed this to the monster?

NO

Then breathe, smile, and throw the paper in the bin.

The Flower

You are like a flower.

Each petal is different, and that's what makes the flower so unique, and so beautiful.

And you, how are you unique? What are your qualities?

Write your name in the middle of the flower, or glue your photo.

Write one of your qualities on each petal. All petals must be filled in.

Then color your flower.

Look at this flower as often as possible. It must be imprinted in your mind.

This flower is you!

My Protective Tattoo

Did you know that in ancient times, tattoos were not just decorative?

According to beliefs, they gave strength and courage, provided protection, or healed the body and mind.

They can be made of drawings, symbols, words.

It's time for you to draw your protective tattoo.

I reassure you, you don't have to really get a tattoo...

And if you don't know how to draw, cut out pictures, make collages.

Volcano

Sometimes (often) we keep our anxieties, our fears, our anger inside us.

We feed our stress and this is a very bad thing.

So, like a volcano, we are going to spit out this burning lava.

Write short sentences or words in the lava of the volcano.

What do you want to say? To whom?

Don't be polite, write what you really think.

Then take this book, go outside and SHOUT everything you've written. If you live in the city or have neighbours right next door get in your car and go for a drive.

Cardiac Coherence

Cardiac coherence is a relaxation method based on breathing.

It allows you to quickly find full serenity, emotional calm and better concentration. It can also help with depression and blood pressure.

When you are relaxed and calm, your heart rhythm is regular and harmonious. You are in "cardiac coherence".

However, when you are stressed, your heart races and its rhythm becomes anarchic. So there is a real connection between your brain and your heart.

The goal is to train yourself to balance your heart rate by following the curve of your breathing, to evacuate your anxiety and self-regulate your emotions.

The method

Sit down with your hands on your legs or on a table, keep your back straight and close your eyes.

Breathe calmly at a rate of six breaths per minute for about five minutes.

It's really very simple, isn't it?

To be practiced without moderation...

The flower does not dream of the bee.

It blossoms and the bee comes.

The Crystal Ball

It's often said that it's important to be in the present moment. And it's true.

But being in the present does not mean not thinking about the future.

Right now you are on a way. The way of your life. But where are you going?

What's your goal?

Think about your ideal future. Don't refrain from dreaming.

Who are you with? Where do you live? What are your activities? And most importantly, who are you? What has changed in you, in your life?

Draw your future in this crystal ball.

Having a goal, a precise objective, helps to regulate anxiety. Why? For several reasons: The first is that you will focus your energy on a precise objective. This will prevent you from focusing on your small worries. The second reason is that having a goal (a real one) strengthens your mind and gives you the courage to overcome your fears. By working on your mind and your self-esteem, you become stronger... And anxiety is reduced.

This is a projection exercise. When you have an goal, visualise it. Imagine that you have achieved it Feel the emotions.

This helps you to develop your creativity, your motivation.

On The Road

Now that you have visualised your ideal future, you will have to walk.

To where?

To your goal. And there are steps along the way.

Take a specific goal that is part of your ideal future.

Visualize it.

What is the way?

What are the steps?

If my goal is to lose weight, I'll have to learn to eat better, change my eating habits, learn to cook differently, do some sport, maybe a bit of swimming first, then move on to fitness or weight training.

If you have a goal and you don't visualise the steps, you will never take action. And you will never reach your goal. Then you'll just sit there and brood.

Draw a road or a stairway. On arrival, write down your goal. And on the way (or on each step of the stairs), write down a stage/step.

IT TAKES A LIFETIME TO LEARN HOW TO LIVE.

My Mantra

A mantra is a spiritual formula that you repeat out loud or in your head when a situation makes you anxious.

This will help you focus your mind on something positive.

How do I create my mantra?

1. Use strong, positive words that have meaning and value to you.

2. Use the present tense to make it fit your current reality,

3. Use the first person singular, always to anchor yourself.

Create your Mantra now

(You can also create several)

Some examples of mantras

I am calm and relaxed. No one can upset me without my consent. I'm fine.

I'm perfect as I am.

I'm free and happy.

I'm here and now.

Nothing can touch me.

Everything is all right.

My Mantra

Time to Worry

We will try to compartmentalize our anxious thoughts instead of keeping them in mind all day.

Take an hourglass, a stopwatch or a mobile phone alarm, and allow yourself one moment of anxiety a day.

No longer than 15 minutes.

During this time, concentrate only on your worries.

When the time is up, you should refrain from thinking about your worries.

If you feel the need, you can give yourself several moments during the day.

Color this drawing, just for fun.

BE A WARRIOR

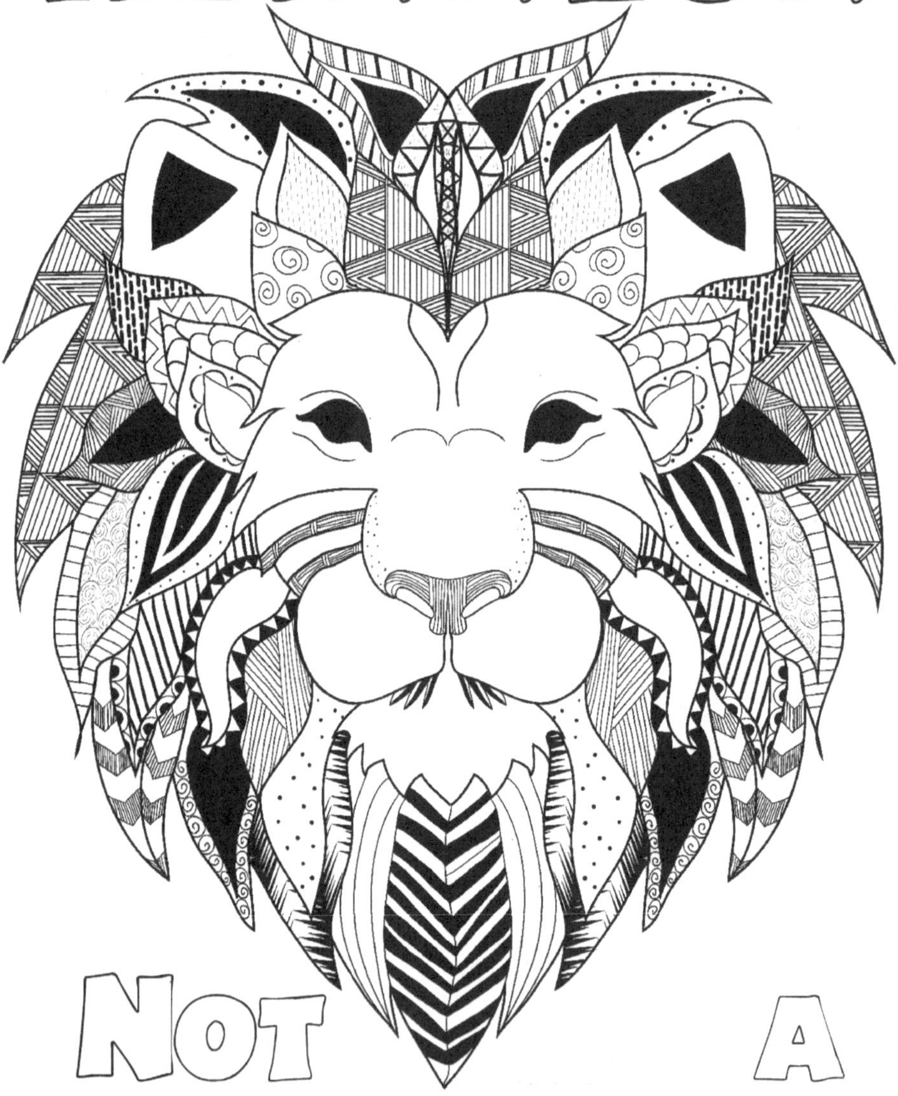

NOT A WORRIER

create your own calm

Paradise

Here's a little exercise to reduce anxiety quickly and feel safe.

You will mentally create your paradise.

Imagine a place, a setting, a landscape. It can be a real place where you feel good, or a place that you have completely invented.

Close your eyes.

What do you hear in this place? Birds? Music?

Is there sunshine? trees? mountains?

Do you see people you know? Or are you alone?

Feel the calm of this place. Feel the calm in you.

No one can enter this place... except you. This is YOUR paradise.

Repeat this exercise once or twice a day, for at least 5 minutes.

When a stressful situation arises, take refuge in your paradise.

This exercise is one of my favourites. It calms my anxiety very quickly.

I will describe my paradise to you: It's a plain, the grass is very green. There is a small river flowing. I can hear the birds, the nature. There is a beautiful sun, like in spring. I'm sitting on a rock near the river and I feel so good.

Draw your paradise, or describe it.

Ho'oponopono

« *The problem is not the reality on the outside, it is on the inside. And to change this reality, we must change ourselves.* » Krishnamurti.

Ho'oponopono is a Hawaiian practice of reconciliation and forgiveness.

According to the principles of Ho'oponopono, everyone is responsible for his or her own life - and therefore for his or her inner peace and actions - and as the creator of what happens to him or her, it is totally unnecessary to try to change others or situations, or to play the victim.

The essence of the Ho'oponopono Method is a simple formula:

Sorry - Please Forgive Me - Thank you - I love you

Try this every time you feel a negative emotion.

Explanations of the formula

Here is what each word means and what it brings us when we recite the formula.

Sorry: We recognize the situation that is happening to us. We observe it and accept it.

Forgive me: We forgive ourselves, others or even the Universe for making us live this conflict. Forgiveness brings liberation for both the giver and the receiver. We do not accuse, we forgive. It is very different. Forgiveness makes it possible to undo the blockage that could arise if we don't do it. We take responsibility for what happens.

Thank you: We make sense of the situation by finding out what it has taught us and what it has allowed us to "clean up". Gratitude helps to initiate positive change.

I love you: In this way, we renew our love instead of remaining in negativity.

My Mask

Often we go through life with a mask. And this mask is sometimes very useful.

Batman wears his mask to frighten his enemies, clown puts on his red nose to make people laugh.

And you, how is your mask? What quality does it reflect? How can it help you in anxious situations?

What emotion does your mask inspire? Fear? kindness and gentleness? what color is it?

Your mask should highlight your qualities, and help you overcome your fears.

This exercise is both fun and can be very effective in certain situations. This "mask" can help you adopt a behavior, a posture better adapted to a situation or a person.

draw your mask

What if it Happens?

Let me tell you: About ten years ago, I left my job to start my own business. And it was a big mistake. For a few months, I was in an incredible state of anxiety, and I kept telling myself: why did I leave my job to do this? I'm a loser. And then, thanks to this flop, I met the boss of a company, who hired me to assist him. I stayed there for a few years and made a lot more money than before.

You know, you can't control everything. And sometimes that's what causes our anxiety.

Our brains start to fear the unknown.

But let's put the consequences in perspective.

You have a business appointment across town and you're afraid of getting lost? What if it happens? Is that so bad?

Your son or daughter has an important exam and you are afraid he or she will fail? What if it happens? Will his or her life be ruined?

Are you afraid your boss will fire you? What if he or she does? There are no other jobs on Earth?

You left your job to create your company and you are afraid to fail?

What if it happens? You won't die! You will be able to do something else. And you will have learned a lot from this experience.

Or even worse...

You are preparing a family meal and you are afraid to burn the turkey? What if it happens? Will they eat you instead?

Most of our stress comes from our incredible ability to imagine the worst, to give too much importance to certain situations.

Whenever you feel anxious, think about it.
What if it happens?

The Worry Tree

Is there something that worries you ?

Write it down on a worrypuff and place it in the worry tree.

Ask yourself : Is there anything I can do about it?

If not, take a green leaf and put it in the tree. Think about something else. One day, that leaf will fall...

If yes, Ask you : What can I do ? When ?

If it's now, take a red leaf, write down your worry and make a plan. And do it ! When it's done, drop that leaf at the base of the tree.

If it's later, take an orange leaf, write your worry and make a plan.

You will find some cutting sheets on the last page.
Color them according to your needs.

My Super Hero Armor

All Heroes have an armor, or a combat suit, or a shield.

Sometimes, life forces us to fight. Not necessarily to fight against others, but mostly to fight against ourselves, against our own fears.

Create your armor!

It should be beautiful, comfortable, and it should look like you.

Draw, glue pictures...

You can also just create a shield, by drawing protection symbols, colors that you like.

Now, imagine that this armour, as well as the mask you created, can fit into an object.

Choose an object that you always carry with you: A ring or a necklace? A pencil? Keys? Anything you like...

Take this object in your hand and mentally put your armour and mask inside. Transfer your superhero powers into this object.

Repeat this visualisation exercise often, and carry this object with you when you have to face an anxious situation.

draw your armor

ABC

The ABC psychological model can help you identify and modify your anxious thoughts.

Here's how it works.

Activating event: The event that will create the anxiety.

Beliefs: You think you are not up to it, that you cannot overcome it.

Consequence: You feel very anxious, depressed.

Disputing: You challenge this belief.

Effect : You feel better, able to overcome this obstacle.

Let's look at an example:

Your boyfriend (or girlfriend) has just left you.

You think that no one else will love you, and that you will end up alone.

You are depressed and you lock yourself away at home.

There are so many people in the world, there must be someone who is right for you, who you will love and who will love you.

You find a smile again, you make yourself beautiful and you go out.

Try the ABC method with 2 current worries.

The Past is the Past

A little anecdote: My son had a bad grade in math recently. So he was very anxious about his upcoming exam.

I asked him: Why did you get a bad grade?

He said: I didn't know my lesson well.

And I said: Well learn it better!

Sometimes we hold on to a past (bad) experience and turn it into an absolute truth.

And in every similar situation, we imagine that the same thing will happen.

In this way we feed our anxiety.

Take a step back, learn from your mistakes and take action.

Example

I'm afraid to go to a job interview.

For what reason? Because the last one went badly and I didn't get the job.

Ok, so I'm going to prepare this interview better, find out more about this company, and do my best.

Now it's your turn!

My Model

Think of someone you think is cool, self-confident. Someone you admire. Someone you would like to look like.

It could be someone you really know, or an actor/actress, a singer or musician, or even a fictional character or superhero.

Got it ?

Close your eyes. What are his or her qualities? The way he or she talks? The way he or she stands? Immerse yourself in this person.

Now think of something that makes you anxious right now. A problem in your relationship? An upcoming business meeting?

Close your eyes. How would your role model act in this situation? What would he or she say? What would he or she do?

This little simulation exercise is very useful in some situations to gain confidence and and act more relaxed.

Glue a photo/picture of
your model

COURAGE IS NOT THE ABSENCE OF FEAR,

BUT THE ABILITY TO OVERCOME IT.

The Boat
Anxiety VS Truth

Let me tell you an anecdote: A few years ago, the company I worked for organised sailing trip. I had never been on a boat at sea before. I was very anxious. In the days leading up to the trip, I kept telling myself, "I'm going to be sick", "this is going to be a terrible day", and "my co-workers are going to laugh at me". I was anxious for days and days.

The day arrived: I took a seasickness medication and got on the boat. We left the port (too late to leave the boat, I guess?). Finally, I sat at the front of the boat, looked out at the sea and the horizon and breathed in the iodized air. I didn't get sick. I may not have had the best day of my life, but it wasn't as bad as I had imagined. In conclusion, I spent days worrying about nothing.

Most of the time we are anxious for wrong reasons. We imagine something and we think it is the truth. This is how we create our anxiety.

Here are a some examples:

You have to conduct a meeting and you think you won't make it?

The truth is, there is no reason for it to go wrong. The only thing you need to do is to prepare properly for the meeting.

You like someone very much, and you don't dare to go and talk to them. You think "He/she will think I am ridiculous".

The truth is that you cannot know what she/he thinks of you. Go ahead, he/she might be the love of your life.

Your wife/husband is 10 minutes late. You start to worry. He/she must have had an accident. Stop right there! The most likely reason is that he/she left work a little late.

Remember, anxiety is not reality. It is the fear of the future, of a hypothetical event that exists only in your imagination.

Anxiety VS Truth

Now that we have realized that what causes our anxiety is not the truth, let's try this exercise.

In the box on the left, write down what makes you anxious.

In the box on the right, write down what is real and true.

On the line below, write an actual action.

This is your turn.

Take your time, this is an important thinking exercise, to become aware of the truth. Use the example below as a guide.

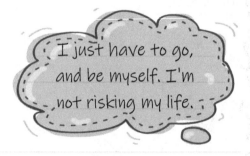

Prepare well for my interview. Be presentable.

The Tornado

Anxiety is often an downward spiral, or a tornado.

You start to feel stressed, so you think about your worries more and more. And you don't do anything else. You think about it again and again, more and more.

Get out of the tornado!

You're going to have to list 10 activities you like to do and that make you feel good.

When you are in the tornado, get out by doing one of these activities.

To help you out, here are some of my favourite activities.

Playing music. Going out for a walk. Doing sports. Doing yoga. Cooking. Watch a movie. Drawing.

My anti-worry activities

BE PROUD OF YOURSELF

STRENGTH
AND WISDOM

The Anchor

In NLP*, creating the anchor is a pattern of response to a stimulus, so that you feel what you want when you need it.

It's a very powerful tool!

Here's how to do it:

1. Determine how you want to feel. For example, be relaxed.

2. Remember a specific moment when you feel really relaxed. Do you have it?

3. Choose an anchoring device that involves touch, for example by touching your thumb and forefinger together or pinching your pinky tip. It should be an easy and discreet gesture.

4. Close your eyes. Remember when you were so relaxed, so good. Where were you? Who were you with? Remember every detail, the sounds, the smells, the heat. Feel the calm of that moment. Now do your anchoring gesture, and continue to feel the happiness of that moment. Stay like this for as long as you like, always with your eyes closed.

5. Repeat this exercise every day for at least 2 weeks. Test it from time to time. If you start to feel anxious, do your anchoring gesture. If you feel better immediately, that's fine. If not, continue doing this exercise every day until the anchor works.

Create your anchor.

*Neuro-linguistic programming (NLP).

Riddikulus !

« He lifted the lid and the lights went out and an icy cold spread. A rattle was heard and a rotten hand reached out to him. » Harry Potter and the Prisoner of Azkaban

A Boggart is an amortal shapeshifting non-being that takes on the form of its observer's worst fear.

Riddikulus is a charm that use to defeat a Boggart. It causes the creature to take on a humorous form for the caster, removing its ability to terrorise.

We all have a boggart, or even several. In the course of our lives, it takes on different forms and faces: Our boss or a colleague, that weird guy you pass every morning on the bus, even your own mother sometimes!

A long time ago, I had a tyrannical manageress. I was young, and she really scared me. I started to imagine her as a little goblin, with make-up and a blonde wig (probably because the Lord of the Ring movie had just come out). Every time she came towards me, I focused on that image. It didn't stop her from being a tyrant, but it helped me feel less afraid.

Draw your Boggart (you can glue a picture of a person, or draw it, or describe it with words),

and make it look ridiculous!

Jin Shin Jyutsu

Jin Shin Jyutsu is a Japanese practice.

To put it simply, each finger is linked to an emotion, and to one or more organs.

To relieve emotions and relax, grasp the finger with the opposite hand, wrapping all the fingers and thumb around it (As if you were holding the handlebars of your bicycle).

Hold the finger firmly for 1 to 2 minutes.

Repeat with each finger OR You can also concentrate on just one finger.

Do the same with the other hand.

For general stress relief, press your thumb into the middle of your hand for 2 minutes.

Do this every day, and every time you feel a negative emotion.

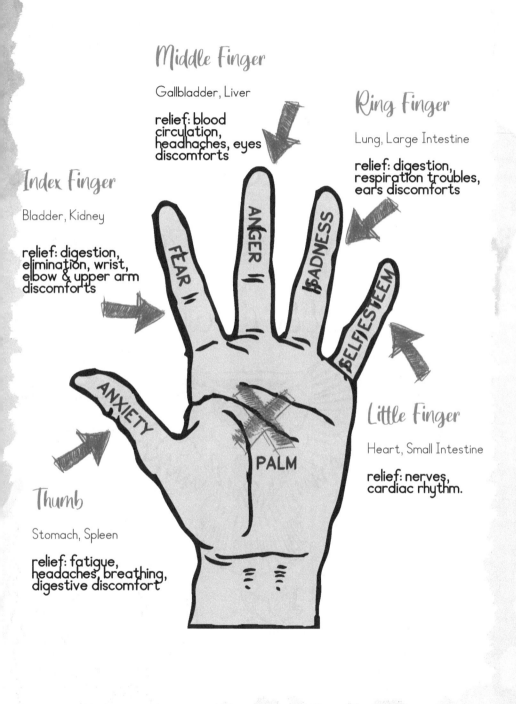

Middle Finger

Gallbladder, Liver

relief: blood circulation, headaches, eyes discomforts

Ring Finger

Lung, Large Intestine

relief: digestion, respiration troubles, ears discomforts

Index Finger

Bladder, Kidney

relief: digestion, elimination, wrist, elbow & upper arm discomforts

Little Finger

Heart, Small Intestine

relief: nerves, cardiac rhythm.

Thumb

Stomach, Spleen

relief: fatigue, headaches, breathing, digestive discomfort

FEAR

ANGER

SADNESS

SELF-ESTEEM

ANXIETY

PALM

the distance between

dreams and reality

is called action

WHOEVER MOVES A MOUNTAIN STARTS WITH A SMALL STONE.

And Now ?

That's it.

You've reached the end.

The end? Really?

No, not really... You'll have to go on alone.

But now you have the tools to manage your anxiety and say "shut up".

You've been able to become aware of your deepest fears, your goals, and most importantly your values and qualities.

You are ready!

Go on with your life serenely, and have confidence in yourself.

The next few pages are for you.

Free expression!

Note your evolution for example. Or talk about situations in which you were able to calm your anxiety.

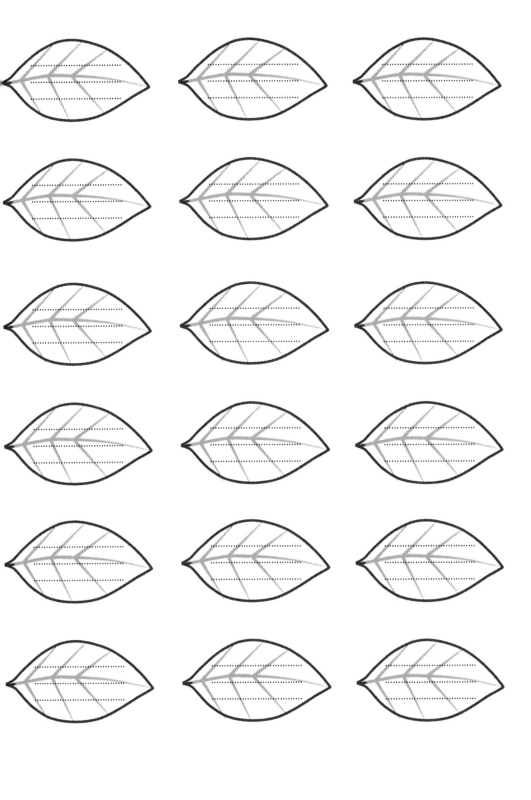

13486393R00066